Predators

Written by Mignonne Gunasekara
Designed by Danielle Rippengill

©Published 2022.
BookLife Publishing Ltd.
King's Lynn, Norfolk PE30 4LS

ISBN 978-1-80155-160-1

All rights reserved. Printed in Poland.
A catalogue record for this book is available
from the British Library.

Predators
Written by Mignonne Gunasekara. Adapted by William Anthony
Designed by Danielle Rippengill

An Introduction to Accessible Readers...

Our 'really readable' Accessible Readers have been specifically created to support the reading development of young readers with learning differences, such as dyslexia.

Our aim is to share our love of books with children, providing the same learning and developmental opportunities to every child.

INCREASED FONT SIZE AND SPACING improves readability and ensures text feels much less crowded.

OFF-WHITE BACKGROUNDS ON MATTE PAPER improves text contrast and avoids dazzling readers.

SIMPLIFIED PAGE LAYOUT reduces distractions and aids concentration.

CAREFULLY CRAFTED along guidelines set out in the British Dyslexia Association's Dyslexia-Friendly Style Guide.

Additional images courtesy of Shutterstock.com. Recurring images – be-bright (arcade floor), behind_green_eyes (arcade wall pattern), RaiDztor (arcade wall texture), vapadi (Ellie's top), sema srinouljan (Ellie's shorts), Offscreen (Professor Molebody's hat). P3 – Nik Merkulov, p6–7 – kasha_malasha, VL1, p8–9 – Skylines, wk1003mike, p10–11 – wk1003mike, p16–17 – wk1003mike, p18–19 – Dean Drobot, ping198, elysart, cluckva, wk1003mike, Kriengsuk Prasroetsung, p26–27 – Alex Leo, Alexander Mazurkevich, Praew stock, p28–29 – Praew, Nik Merkulov.

Contents

Page 4	Meet the Predators
Page 6	Lion
Page 8	Bald Eagle
Page 10	Great White Shark
Page 12	Alligator Snapping Turtle
Page 14	King Cobra
Page 16	Great White Pelican
Page 18	Red-Bellied Piranha
Page 20	Nile Crocodile
Page 22	Orca
Page 24	Peregrine Falcon
Page 26	Komodo Dragon
Page 28	Polar Bear
Page 30	Index
Page 31	Predators: Quiz

Meet the Predators

Welcome to the world of predators. Predators are animals that hunt other animals, called prey, for food. They all have something in common – to their prey, they are terrifying!

All sorts of animals can be predators. We will look at mammals, reptiles, fish and birds. Some of them may look cute or cool, but all of them are deadly hunters.

Lion

Lions are big cats that live in a family group called a pride. Female lions often do most of the hunting for the pride.

Lions usually hunt at night, using their sharp teeth and claws. They can work together to hunt animals much bigger than they are. Lions often steal food from other predators.

Bald Eagle

Bald eagles are a type of bird. They have very good eyesight and can see prey from far away. Eagles have sharp beaks that help them to rip into food.

Bald eagles use their talons to grab fish out of the water. Bald eagles eat a lot of fish, such as salmon. They also steal prey that other animals have killed.

Great White Shark

The great white shark is the largest predator on Earth that is a fish.
It can grow to be six metres long.
It has a strong sense of smell.

Great white sharks eat all sorts of other animals, such as fish, seals and sea lions. Great whites have over 300 teeth to catch prey with.

Alligator Snapping Turtle

Alligator snapping turtles are some of the largest turtles in the world. These turtles hunt for prey by using something called a lure. The lure looks like a worm.

The alligator snapping turtle sits still and wiggles the red lure on its tongue. When prey gets close to have a look, the turtle snaps its mouth shut and eats it!

King Cobra

King cobras can lift the front part of their bodies off the ground while moving forward. They do this to frighten off animals that are scaring them. Scared cobras spread out their hoods and hiss.

The king cobra kills prey with venom. Venom is a dangerous thing that some animals can inject into others. The king cobra's main prey is other snakes. King cobras can even climb trees and swim.

Great White Pelican

Pelicans are some of the largest birds on Earth. They are known for the stretchy pouches under their bills, which they use to scoop fish out of the water.

Great white pelicans usually hunt for fish in groups. They swim together and push the fish into one area, then scoop them up to eat.

Red-Bellied Piranha

Red-bellied piranhas have sharp, triangular teeth. They also have an amazing sense of hearing and can hear prey from far away. Piranhas can also smell blood from far away too.

Red-bellied piranhas are scavengers. This means they eat what they can find and don't always kill their own prey. Sometimes they will even eat plants.

Nile Crocodile

Adult Nile crocodiles are apex predators. This means that they don't have any predators hunting them. Nile crocodiles are known to eat whatever prey they can find.

Nile crocodiles even eat prey as large as wildebeest, small hippos and zebras. They have also been known to attack humans that get too close to them.

Orca

Orcas are also known as killer whales. They live in family groups called pods. Orcas are very clever. Pods can work together to take down giant prey, such as whales.

An orca can make sounds that travel underwater until they hit an object, such as a prey animal. The sounds then bounce back to the orca. This tells the orca where the object is. This is called echolocation.

Peregrine Falcon

Peregrine falcons can be found everywhere, from cliffs by the sea to tall buildings in cities. A peregrine falcon's main prey is birds.

Peregrine falcons hunt by diving at their prey while in the air. They can reach speeds of over 300 kilometres per hour while diving. This makes them the fastest animal in the world!

Komodo Dragon

The Komodo dragon is the largest lizard in the world. It will eat whatever prey it can find. It hunts large animals such as deer and water buffalo.

Komodo dragons wait for prey to come close to them before attacking. If prey gets away, Komodo dragons will follow it until it dies and then eat it.

Polar Bear

Polar bears have large front paws that help them to swim. They are the largest carnivores to live on land and their main prey is seals.

Polar bears hunt by waiting near gaps in the ice for a seal to pop up. They also eat dead animals they find, such as whales.

Index:

birds 5, 8–9, 16–17, 24–25

families 6, 22

fish 5, 9–11, 16–19

mammals 5–7, 21–23, 26, 28–29

reptiles 5, 12–15, 20–21, 26–27

water 9, 16, 23

Predators: Quiz

1. Which animals in this book hunt in groups or families?

2. The fastest animal in the world is in this book. What is its name?

3. What is a lure?

4. Using the index, can you find a page with information about water?

5. Which animal was your favourite predator? How does it hunt for prey?

Helpful Hints for Reading at Home

This 'really readable' Accessible Reader has been carefully written and designed to help children with learning differences whether they are reading in the classroom or at home. However, there are some extra ways in which you can help your child at home.

- Try to provide a quiet space for your child to read, with as few distractions as possible.

- Try to allow your child as much time as they need to decode the letters and words on the page.

- Reading with a learning difference can be frustrating and difficult. Try to let your child take short, managed breaks between reading sessions if they begin to feel frustrated.

- Build your child's confidence with positive praise and encouragement throughout.

- Your child's teacher, as well as many charities, can provide you with lots of tips and techniques to help your child read at home.